Stephen Woodhams

innovative
flower
arrangements
for all
occasions

photography by Lorry Eason
Quadrille

First published in 1998 by

Quadrille Publishing Limited

Alhambra House, 27–31 Charing Cross Road, London WC2H 0LS

Creative Director Mary Evans

Editorial Director Jane O'Shea

Art Director Françoise Dietrich

Project Editor Hilary Mandleberg

Production Vincent Smith, Candida Jackson

Photography by Lorry Eason

*To Nature, the mother of my inspiration...
to my aunts, Belle & Freda...
and to the beauty of flowers.*

British Library Cataloguing-in-Publication Data
A catalogue record for this book is available from the British Library.

ISBN 1 899988 03 3

Printed and bound by KHL Printing, Singapore

contents

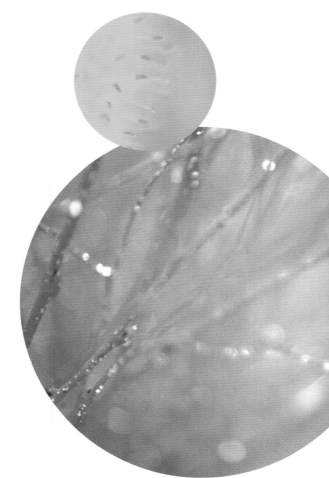

dedicated to the one I love

Flowers are what I really love best so, in a way, this book is dedicated to them for all the joy they have brought me. I feel truly lucky to be thinking about and working with flowers all day long. They can do so many things. They can set the scene for a celebration, be a way of saying I love you, thank you, or I'm sorry, or they can simply just be there to lift the spirits. Sometimes, if I'm having a dinner party and I'm in a panic about the food or who should sit where, I find that arranging the flowers for the table is a great way to relax. Or, when I get home after a hard day, just arranging a few flowers for myself in a favourite vase quickly enables me to unwind.

Being a floral decorator is not the easiest occupation in the world. I have to work very long hours, starting at the flower market at three in the morning and often helping to put the finishing touches to the flowers for a party at four in the afternoon – thirteen hours later! But even though I am now running a large business, and have a wonderful team of people to help and support me in my relentless search for perfection and in my love of all things natural, I still feel there is no substitute for choosing my own flowers. It gives me the chance to make last-minute, perhaps unexpected combinations, and the end-result is so rewarding that, even after ten years, I find it just as exciting as when I began.

The other excitements for me of being in this business are the opportunity to meet so many people who share my passion for flowers, and the chance to add my own artistic statement to what are often stunningly aesthetic locations in their own right – great old houses, beautiful churches or chapels, magnificent banqueting halls or slickly contemporary conference centres.

Because of my other passion – for good food – some of my best experiences have been working with great chefs in their restaurants. Like a good meal, a good flower arrangement should leave you feeling happy and satisfied. In fact, that's not the only similarity so I like to follow the example of a friend who also happens to be a brilliant London chef. She firmly believes that foods are at their best when in season, so would never, for example, use strawberries except in summer. It's the same with my flower arranging. I try to stick to what's in season, avoiding tulips until spring, roses until summer, and berries until the autumn. Go with nature and the chances are, you will rarely get it wrong.

At the end of the day I hope, through this book, to share with you my passion for flowers, a characteristic I attribute to my grandfather who was a nurseryman. Like me, he realised that one of the great things about flowers is that they do not recognise any class distinctions. Even the simplest ones can bring joy to our lives, whatever our background. I hope, too, that by reading this book, you will gain some ideas and confidence to help you arrange your flowers in a way that you can be proud of. But, more than anything, I hope you will have as much fun with flowers as I do.

up, up & away

the fundamentals of flower arranging

Have you ever bought some flowers that caught your eye and put them in your favourite vase in the living room, only to find that they just didn't look as good as you expected? What about the time you saw a terrific container at a friend's house, bought the same one, brought it home and it looked awful?

The reason for these sometimes expensive mistakes is that every room, every container, even every flower, has its own character. A successful arrangement will be one that brings together those elements that have similar characters, though, if you are lucky enough to have an eye for them, unexpected combinations can be the most successful of all. Colour, of course, is the other main element in an arrangement, so it's also important to know how colours affect one another. With a bit of practice, you'll soon get a feel for what looks right.

As well as giving some tips on the mechanics of flower arranging, I can't resist recommending my very favourite flowers, foliage and plants – tomorrow's classics. Some of these are just so fabulous that, to my mind, they will go on looking great and being chosen for flower arranging for many years to come.

good vibrations

What is it that makes some flower arrangements work and give out good vibrations, while others simply miss the point? Most of us can look at an arrangement and immediately know if it's successful or not, if it makes the impact that's intended. But not all of them hit the mark. Although some people have an instinctive flair for flower arranging, most of the greatest arrangements haven't happened by chance. They've been worked on long and hard. Their success has a lot to do with the sensitive combination of the style of the flowers with their setting – more of that later – but the first impact of an arrangement is usually made by its colour.

I am passionate about colour. It's such an important part of our lives. Anyone is sure to remember the impact of an all-red arrangement in an all-white room, or the brightness that a crate of sunflowers will bring to a summer garden-party table, or the clarity of a white arum lily – even though white is not, strictly speaking, a colour but an amalgam of all the colours of the rainbow.

Colour preferences are very personal, and what one person likes, another will absolutely loathe. This is due partly to the way we associate different things with different colours. Some of us think of green as the colour of the countryside and of soothing nature, while others associate it with the greens they had to eat as a child. For certain people, blue suggests the sky and the sea. I sometimes associate it with the colour of my hated maths textbook. Red can bring to mind drama and passion, or it can conjure up blood and carnage, while yellow might recall happy memories of childhood seaside holidays with sunshine and sand, or the ghastly faded yellow paintwork of one's first rented flat.

All these single colours are fairly straightforward, but things really get interesting when we start putting different colours next to one another, and that's where a bit of technical know-how doesn't come amiss. Basically, as well as the three primary colours – red, blue and yellow – the spectrum includes three secondaries – green, orange and violet – as well as all the shades in between. Some of the colours of the spectrum are warm and some are cool. We usually think of blues and greens as cool, and of reds and yellows as warm, but there are plenty of blues that veer towards purple and so have a touch of warmth about them, just as there are plenty of acid-yellows that are very definitely on the cool side thanks to the bit of green in their make-up.

If you are looking for a harmonious colour scheme, whether it's in choosing clothes, for a flower arrangement or for decorating a

room, the trick is to put together colours of approximately the same temperature. A cool harmony, for instance, that will make you feel relaxed and calm, could be made up of clear minty greens, grey-greens and acid-greens. For a summer wedding-table centre, I might make a container of green apples filled with lush green and grey-green foliage, clumps of lady's mantle, cream stocks and lilies. All-foliage arrangements can also make cool harmonies, with the differing shapes and textures of the leaves adding to the effect, while clear, icy blues and mauves – combinations of lisianthus, irises, cornflowers, love-in-a-mist, salvias and thistles – are also great. For warm harmonies, go for reds, oranges and yellows – amaryllis, crocosmia, dahlias, roses, rudbeckias, gladioli, ornamental peppers – the list is endless. I must say that one of my favourite warm harmony combinations is made up of orange and yellow – the orange and yellow roses on page 50 or a mass of orange and yellow marigolds. Harmonies made up of these colours will be far from restful, but if you include cooled-down tints of reds, oranges and yellows – pinks, pale oranges and yellows – the effect will veer towards cool and calming again.

A sizzling combination of tulips in warm burgundy, yellow and orange with cool purple will bring any room to life with its powerful intensity of colour.

What beats the pazzazz of purple and orange? What packs more of a punch than turquoise and tangerine? What stops you in your tracks if not red and green? For drama like this in your flower arrangements, contrasts are a must.

A contrast is made when two complementary colours are put next to one another. On the colour wheel – a visual often used for classifying colour – complementary colours stand opposite one another. Since the colour wheel also has warm and cool colours opposite one another, a true contrast will be a contrast of temperature as well as one of colour. Put two complementaries next to each other and, for rather technical reasons, each will enhance the effect of the other. So in a combination of orange gerberas with lime-green lady's mantle, the orange will look even more orange, and the lime-green more strongly green. That's part of what makes contrasts so powerful.

To make the story more complicated, you can also have contrasts of tone – the lightness or darkness of a colour. Think of deep purple violas and pale narcissi, for instance. Or deep purple heuchera with pale green bells of Ireland. White gives the most intense contrasts of tone with any colour, simply because nothing comes paler than white but, strangely enough, the strongest contrasts actually come from colours that are closest in tone – somehow this closeness emphasises the colour difference even more. The red berries of holly contrast brilliantly with the green of its foliage. Clear red geraniums sing out against their bright green leaves.

wild thing

Then there are the colour contrasts that really shock with their audacity. Scarlet, pink and orange. Purple, orange and blue. Purple, orange and red. Use these if you dare. Their strength comes from the fact that they seem to be harmonious mixes of colours, but in fact use colours of different temperatures. That's what really gives them something to shout about. Purple lisianthus will set white flowers alight, but put the cool lisianthus with warm red or orange gerberas, and you'll get a real conflagration. Cool blue and white flowers are a classic combination, but add hot spots of purple and orange for maximum vibrancy. The heat is on!

RIGHT AND BELOW
The graphic shape of silvery-
blue globe thistles reminds me
of craters on the moon, while
the soft opening buds and
knobbly twigs of the flowering
prunus have a very country feel.

come together

In my work as a professional designer, the starting-point for most of my flower arrangements or installations is usually a specific location, often with a particular occasion in mind. For instance, I might be asked to do the flowers for a society wedding, for a gathering of politicians at a conference centre, or for a dear friend's birthday party. Certain locations and occasions usually suggest a specific style, mood or atmosphere. A bunch of flowers laid in a trug and looking as if they have been freshly picked from the garden would not be appropriate to grace the table at a gathering of businessmen, nor would a single stem of the bold, graphic heliconia look good in a cosy, beamed living room in the depths of the country.

Broadly speaking, styles of arrangements fall into just three categories – the country look, the classic look and contemporary, or urban, chic. Formality and informality are factors to be taken into account too. Nowadays informality holds sway. We see far less of the stiffly formal style of flower arranging that was common in the seventies and eighties. That is obvious even in the way florists make up bouquets today. Now they are usually presented hand-tied and wrapped in brown parcel paper or clear cellophane, sometimes with a piece of coloured, toning tissue paper as well. Gone, thank heavens, are those huge, ugly, flat bouquets that look more suitable for laying on a coffin than for giving as a birthday present or as a gift to celebrate the birth of a child.

Often there is some overlap between the different styles and formality and informality. For instance, if I put a mass of single-coloured wallflowers – a typical cottage-garden flower – into a galvanised pot they become unexpectedly contemporary, and the more so if I have cut them all to the same length. What is normally seen as an informal, loose-looking, country-style flower is suddenly given a modern twist. In a similar vein, if I combine arum lilies – one of the great classics of the flower world – with some vivid green stems of bamboo, and finish them off with a collar of anthurium leaves around the neck of the vase, I shall have created something rather startling. It is this element of the unexpected that is so much a feature of my flower arranging and that gives it, I think, its modern edge. It is also what makes choosing and arranging flowers so exciting for me.

For most people, either the flowers they grow in their garden or the ones they can buy from their local florist will be the starting-point and can dictate the style of an arrangement. You might go out to buy stately lilies, but return with a homely bunch of anemones. To my mind, flowers with a rounded, loose appearance, such as roses, sweet peas, campanulas, scabious, cornflowers, poppies and peonies, have an informal, country feel to them, while for a formal, modern look, I would choose strongly graphic, often spiky or abstract-looking flowers or foliage – irises, globe artichokes, bells of Ireland, amaryllis, gladioli, arum lilies, heliconia, agapanthus, gerberas, strelitzias or snapdragons (another cottage-garden flower but now commercially produced to make a flower with stronger, more graphic lines than the garden-grown specimens). These architectural plants and flowers usually look best on

Don't go for the obvious. The owner of this house was expecting a formal arrangement of roses, lilies and foliage for the console table in the hall. Instead, I chose the more audacious alternative of stripes of orange and yellow roses in a rough wooden tray.

their own, or with only one other type of flower or foliage. In fact, it is generally true that varieties used by themselves will look more contemporary, while mixtures are more traditional looking.

But these are not hard and fast rules. A flower can suggest many different things depending on the way it is used. Take roses, for instance. Usually they are associated with the countryside, romance and informality. You only have to look at the straw hat garlanded with large, blowsy roses on page 138 to see what I mean. But change to commercially grown roses, with their small, evenly matched heads and their stems all the same length, put them in a plain, frosted glass vase in an urban living room, and you have an undeniable example of contemporary urban chic. It is the same with lilies. Used on their own, these look very crisp and modern, but mixed with other flowers, they add a touch of classicism to any arrangement. Delphiniums are another example. Usually thought of as traditional cottage-garden plants, they take on a crisp, modern look when massed together in shades of blue (see page 64). Mixed with white flowers they have a classic feel, while in a mixed arrangement with other cottage-garden flowers, they project a country image. Foxtail lilies are similar. Combined with other flowers in a huge urn (see page 52), they look very classic, but on their own, with just a few big leaves, they become unexpectedly modern and very urban.

Your choice of container is another important factor. You should possess as big a selection as possible, as the container can make all the difference to a design. The bold flowers that suit contemporary interiors will make the main statement and here the container should be plain and simple, so there is no vying for attention. Try a mass of huge white agapanthus in a clear glass vase with bold swiss cheese leaves (see page 120), or a single paphiopedilum orchid in a clear glass bowl, or a white phalaenopsis orchid with a stem of contorted willow in a creamware pot. Another stunning idea for a contemporary urban environment would be a mass of white tulips – among my favourite flowers – in a simple green vase, or white gerberas in frosted glass (see page 113). Contemporary locations also suit industrial-looking containers, such as concrete blocks (see page 84), metal rods lined with blown glass (see page 82), or test tubes, either used singly (see page 92) or linked together in a metal frame (see pages 46 and 134).

For traditional arrangements, go for the classic, rounded shapes of urns in glass, metal, porcelain or stone – a tall, frosted goblet-shaped vase filled with romantic summer flowers in harmonising shades (see page 100), or a glass urn filled with tightly packed heads of a single type of rose, without any foliage except, perhaps, a collar of leaves around the neck of the vase – or for vases made

LEFT

Containers come in an enormous variety of shapes and sizes. Old pewter jugs are full of character and look great even without any flowers. So does the simple nickel-plated vase. It is almost a work of art in its own right. The wooden crate filled with lupins and the pair of creamware pots make a totally different kind of statement.

My vase collection is continually growing. I have lots of favourites, though I must say these can change from season to season, depending on the flowers I am working with. It's always nice to see their stems through clear glass, but the disadvantage, of course, is that as soon as the water gets murky, it shows. When that happens, change it. It's better for the flowers and on the eye.

The bold simplicity of a handful of yellow arum lilies in a plain glass vase complements the abstract painting in the background.

of creamware, another design classic that is making a comeback. Pottery jugs, pewter, coloured glass and baskets all make good containers for country-style arrangements, and don't forget the possibilities of simple wooden trugs or crates for informal arrangements of cut flowers or plants (see pages 42, 55 and 111).

Once you have a good collection of containers, you will quickly realise that some of them can be used in a variety of ways. A glass salad bowl could, when not needed for salad, be used for flower arrangements. Place a ring of florist's foam round the top and stud it with flowers, foliage and candles, then fill the centre with water and night-lights (see page 130). You can use the same container with an inner, plastic bowl. Line the space between the glass and the plastic with orange slices and vivid green moss, and fill the plastic bowl with a mass of harmonising flowers. Another idea is to line the glass bowl with whole lemons, and plant the

plastic bowl with yellow ranunculus, or to line it with pebbles, lichen and driftwood and place a smaller glass bowl in the centre filled with red anemones and small cherry tomatoes. Now we're back to salad again!

At the end of the day, when you bring everything together, you must come back to your room setting. A wood-panelled dining room could be crying out for a classical metal urn filled with assorted flowers and foliage in the style of an old Dutch still-life painting. These old paintings aimed to show the widest possible variety of fruits and flowers, rather like botanical records and regardless of whether or not they were all in season at the same time – something that it is relatively easy to emulate nowadays, when so many fruits and flowers are available in the shops for twelve months of the year. To achieve this look, I would choose stately flowers such as crown imperials, Parrot tulips and 'Stargazer' lilies, and mix them with the more country-style old-fashioned pinks, purple lilac, foxgloves, peonies and clusters of roses. Then I would wire some grapes into the front of the arrangement, and would strew cascades of apples, pears, and more grapes around the foot of the urn.

As a complete contrast, the most breathtaking addition to a minimalist living room, containing nothing more than a couple of sofas, a coffee table and a huge, abstract painting, might be just a plain glass vase of yellow arum lilies, their curvy stems tied with a piece of raffia to create a perfect echo of the painting behind. What can you think of that would be more simple, yet more beautiful and more appropriate?

The exquisite texture and colour of this rusty urn in a classic shape work so well with the flowers and ornaments on the mantelpiece that they seem made for each other. The mellow, aged look of the urn adds to the elegance of the setting.

a little help from my friends

Loose, arching stems of bear grass in a narrow-necked vase almost look like a crazy hairstyle gone mad. They will add an exciting sense of movement to any arrangement.

foliage & berries

Having trained as a gardener, I feel very strongly about foliage. I was always taught that, in garden design, the key features apart from the hard landscaping are the trees and shrubs. These form the backdrop to the flowers. I like to think of my flower arrangements in the same way and, unless an arrangement is to be very minimalist, I usually start with at least three different types of foliage. The choice is not as narrow as you might think, and many kinds can easily be grown in your own garden.

For an arrangement of strong, bold colours, I use dark green foliage as a counterbalance. Some of my favourites are *Viburnum tinus*, myrtle, mexican orange and camellia. For white flowers, which might be overwhelmed by strong greens, choose variegated foliage such as pittosporum, or lime-green types – for instance, *Euphorbia polychroma*. For pinks and blues, nothing looks better than foliage from the silver-grey palette. Here the choice is wide. Try whitebeam, or one of the many varieties of eucalyptus. One of my favourite foliage plants is *Brachyglottis* 'Sunshine', which has wonderful silver-grey leaves with a white margin and underside. I also like to use rosemary and the silvery spider's web-type leaves of the globe artichoke. If you are working with rich, burnt oranges and yellows, go for foliage with the same warmth of colour. Choose copper beech, smoke tree, or berries such as ash or *Viburnum tinus*. Another unusual choice would be the beautiful arching seed-heads of crocosmia.

Certain berries and foliage are my first choice in special situations. The burgundy-red berries of hypericum, for example, make a superb base for a hand-tied bouquet in shades of red. I love using ivy, too, not only when I need some trailing strands in an arrangement, but also for its individual leaves which look great with night-lights standing on top of them for a party. For a contemporary tablescape, I often use banana leaves cut into geometric shapes and placed beneath sections of bamboo stems to make candle-holders. Exquisitely aromatic laurel leaves are great glued around a plastic pot, for lining glass dishes, or with winter foliage in a Christmas arrangement. Dried, they can be used for a kitchen display with a culinary theme.

Grasses, like the vivid green bear grass, are becoming ever more popular. Their graphic simplicity makes them ideal for contemporary arrangements. I also love using papyrus heads submerged in water, or fresh wheat with its blue plumes. The water-loving horsetail is another star. You can make containers out of it, or use it to add a touch of originality to a hand-tied bouquet or as a decorative support for flowering plants. Finally, tropical plants, many of which were not brought to the West until the nineteenth century, are being used more and more today. Their highly graphic appearance means that they usually look best on their own. One of my favourites is the swiss cheese plant. Its dramatic foliage is so unusual, it's hard to believe it's real.

plants

Because they are long-lasting, I use plants whenever I can. They also give me the opportunity to do something a bit different. Once I stumbled across a crate of lupins in mixed colours awaiting delivery at a nursery. They looked so wonderful I couldn't think of anything better than copying the idea, so I planted up a mass of them in a polythene-lined crate as a centrepiece for a summer buffet table. I also get a thrill from watching bulbs slowly come into bloom. Stately amaryllis, available mostly in red, pink and white, are such good value. They look great in a modern container or in a rustic wooden box, and they last well. They are terrific as their tall, chunky stems reach for the sky and their fat flower buds slowly unfurl into wonderful, exotic-looking flowers. Hyacinths are very versatile too, and have the bonus of their wonderful scent. For an arrangement with urban chic, I would fill a low, galvanised dish with white hyacinth bulbs, but for a country look I would plant them in a plain wooden container with fine grass growing on top. In fact, grass is another useful plant. Nothing looks more funky than a shallow wooden box lined with polythene

Mosses and lichens are a must. I sometimes use them on their own, but mostly as extras. Different types of moss lend themselves to different situations. To make a moss garland to disguise an otherwise ordinary container, I use shaggy, green sphagnum moss. The compact look of bun moss is great for top-dressing a planted arrangement, while grey, sponge-like lichen suits contemporary compositions, especially in galvanised containers. For an arrangement with a tropical feel, I would usually choose Spanish moss, which is grey with a shredded, hair-like texture.

I love using growing plants in my arrangements. For one thing, they last a lot longer than cut flowers, and for another there is the fun of watching them grow. Ivy is not a fussy plant, and will often grow in poor light where other plants would simply give up and die. It looks especially good trained around a frame to make an indoor topiary. Here I have combined it with some thick twigs for extra interest.

and filled with a piece of cultivated turf. This 'grass panel' would be great in a minimalist interior, as would one made of sprouting grains of wheat. These come up such a vivid green and last about a week indoors.

Orchids are classic plants, but don't just display them in the pot they come in. Phalaenopsis orchids are wonderful either in old terracotta, creamware or galvanised pots, or in glass containers, perhaps with silver sand and shells to give them a nautical theme. x *Vuylstekeara* cambria orchids, especially the wonderful burgundy and white or yellow and brown forms, are also strong contenders. The yellow and brown ones have a truly autumnal feel when planted in a Perspex container lined with corn.

Cacti are becoming increasingly popular now, and come in a wider range of sizes than ever before. They work well in contemporary, minimalist locations and need very little maintenance, which makes them a good buy for people with busy lives. If you are looking for larger, structural plants, some of the cacti would fit the bill, or I would recommend the plaited-stem weeping fig.

Topiary trees add yet another range of possibilities. Choose from standard rosemary, olive, azalea, or *Magnolia stellata* trees, all of which, although usually grown outdoors, can be brought inside for a while. Don't forget, too, the possibilities of ivy topiaries. These can be trained as standard trees, pyramids, globes or basket shapes. Ready-made ones are rather expensive to buy because of all the care that has gone into them, but they are not difficult to train yourself.

A few other favourites of mine include the sixties-style money plant growing in a glass dish with pebbles. Like mind-your-own-business, this is a very clean-cut plant that makes a strong impact in any room. And finally, don't forget plants that not only flower, but have beautiful leaves. The peace lily is one of these. It looks stunning, showing off its dark green leaves and white sails for almost twelve months of the year.

dried flowers

Dried flowers are no longer relegated to some dusty corner of a country cottage. The range of dried material is better now than it has ever been, and this has helped to bring dried arrangements to the forefront of flower arranging. Drying methods now include freeze-drying at many degrees below zero. This keeps the natural bright colours of the flowers and fruit and, when they are used in arrangements, they take back some moisture from the air, which gives them a very life-like appearance.

Instead of using an old-fashioned jumble of dried flowers, the contemporary approach is to use a mass of one flower – domes of dried roses in simple containers, plain glass containers filled with pot-pourri and topped with dried lavender heads, stems of lavender edged with red roses, or different shades of pink and red peonies in old terracotta pots. For a contemporary kitchen, for instance, I would line a glass container with dried peas or corn, and top it off with a dome of ears of dried wheat. Or a rustic panel of woven twigs would look great with a collection of old terracotta pots wired on, together with a few wooden kitchen utensils and some sachets of dried herbs.

Dried-flower mirror frames are another of my favourites. Those made of a mass of dried, assorted flowers (see page 126), remind me of the work of Grinling Gibbons, that master of late seventeenth- and early eighteenth-century woodcarving. They would suit a classic interior. For contemporary appeal, though, you can't beat a mirror edged with tuffets of bun moss or, for the bathroom, try a mirror edged with glued-on shells accompanied by wired-in creamware pots filled with phalaenopsis orchids.

Sculptured trees are another use for dried material. Use stems of silver birch or bamboo poles, to which you fix florist's foam studded with bun moss, dried box, heads of dried flowers, or even dried palm leaves. For a modern twist, I sometimes wrap the stems of these trees in steel cable. 'Cloud trees', with their oriental feel, are similar to sculptured trees. Their 'suspended' clusters of flower heads or moss resemble clouds in the sky. Both these types of 'tree' have something of the quality of a piece of art.

For long-lasting arrangements, you should follow a few simple tips. Firstly, give your flowers and foliage a good deep drink of clean water, preferably overnight, removing all the lower leaves so they do not start rotting. Wrap long, floppy-stemmed plants like tulips and gerberas in paper first to help prevent them from bending.

Certain stems need to be specially treated. Woody ones used to be crushed with a hammer, but it's now thought that this does more harm than good because it makes the stems susceptible to bacterial attack. Instead, cut them at a 45-degree angle to expose the largest possible surface area to the water. Hollow-stemmed plants like amaryllis have a tendency to collapse. To avoid this, place thin canes up the stems, fill them with water, plug them with cotton wool and secure the ends with elastic bands. I use a lot of spurge in my flower arranging, and these ooze a white liquid from their stems every time they are cut. Before you put them in an arrangement, leave them standing in a bucket of water so that the milky liquid runs out, otherwise they will turn the water cloudy. Many other soft-stemmed plants, such as poppies, can be prevented from wilting if their stems are sealed, either by singeing with a naked flame, or by holding them in shallow boiling water for a few seconds. First wrap the flowers up in stiff paper to protect them from the steam. Roses also last longer if they have their stems immersed in boiling water for a few seconds.

Whenever possible, I try to arrange my flower displays in fresh water as they last longer than in wet florist's foam. Sometimes this is not practical though, for instance in an arrangement for a wall-hanging or a pew-end in a church. For these, I try to use mostly woody-stemmed plants that hold up well in foam, rather than fleshy-stemmed ones like hyacinths.

Next, we come to the arrangement itself. The base of a classic arrangement is the foliage. It gives the shape, so is hugely important, and I would always use at least three different varieties. Sometimes I end up with five or more and then think that to add flowers would spoil the effect, so I end up making another composition for the flowers! Lilies are a must for a classic arrangement and they should follow the foliage. After that, add the spiky flowers and then the fillers placed in drifts of odd numbers – three, five or seven stems at a time. Finally I add clusters of my 'star performers' – round-headed flowers like roses, gerberas or peonies. The finished result should look like a section of a herbaceous border, with its interesting colour mixes and variety of shape and form. Modern, graphic designs need a different approach of course, but I still stick to using odd numbers of flowers and foliage.

help!

For some designs you need to use wiring. This can range from something as simple as chicken wire to support large, heavy stems, to the individual wiring-up of fruits or vegetables (see page 48). Often, if I am making an arrangement of flowering plants, I finish it off with tuffets of bun moss pinned down with hairpin-shaped wires. Wiring really comes into its own at Christmas, when nearly everything is wired – clumps of blue spruce, fir cones and walnuts – often helped by a little dab of glue for extra support. I'll only wire flowers as a desperate last resort, though. For instance, if a gerbera insists on bending I might insert a wire into the back of its head and wrap it round the stem, but on the whole I believe that flowers should be left to do their own thing and not be messed around with.

One very artificial type of flower arrangement is the sculptured tree. For this you will need to cement the stem or stems into a plastic pot, then fit this into the final display pot. If you try cementing the stem into a porcelain pot, the cement will expand and crack the porcelain as it dries. You should make sure that any moss you use for these trees is completely dry because if there is any moisture left in it, it will travel along the stems of any dried flowers you use and make them rot.

Rose

Roses form a very large genus of around 125 species. Old garden roses are among my favourite flowers because of their shape and fragrance. Cultivated varieties are invaluable for their many useful colours. Some of these – for instance *R.* 'Ecstasy' and *R.* 'Jacaranda' – are fragrant too.

Flowering prunus

These flowers always remind me of spring. Long before the leaves emerge, their blossom is the first sign of life after winter. The pale pink *P. x subhirtella* 'Autumnalis' can flower as early as December or January.

Flowering prunus

Nearly all the flowering prunus originated in Japan. They often appear in old Japanese prints and drawings.

Nerine

Named after Nerine the water-nymph, this beautiful flower originally came from South Africa. Its elegant flower heads, many from a central stem, are produced before the leaves. The hybrid varieties range from shades of pale pink and white to hot pinks, reds, lilacs and purples.

tomorrow's classics

Belladonna lily

Related to the amaryllis, the belladonna lily is a bulb that is native to South Africa and usually flowers between August and October. Its rich, soapy smell is one of my favourite flower fragrances. It is mostly found in this stunning pink, but is also beautiful in white.

Bells of Ireland

A lovely annual which, although it can be problematic, may be grown from seed for the front of a border. In the garden it grows multi-stemmed, rather than with the single slender stems it has when grown commercially.

Bells of Ireland

One of my favourite green flowers, it works well on its own for a clean, modern look, or as part of a mixed arrangement. Spiky and structural, it also makes a good dried flower.

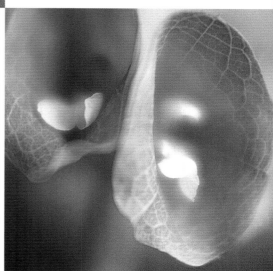

Gerbera

Named after the eighteenth-century German naturalist Traugott Gerber, the gerbera is wonderful, either by itself or as the highlight of a mixed arrangement. It is also great as a house plant. Do not overwater, and it will produce flowers for months.

Gerbera

This dark burgundy variety – 'Chateau' – with its golden eye, is one of the most stunning. Among my other favourites are the bright orange 'Tennessee', and the golden-yellow 'Dallas'.

...flowers

Heliconia

This family comes from South America. The tropical blooms are very bold and dramatic, great for a minimalist treatment as well as with a mass of other flowers. One of my favourites, with its red and yellow hanging flowers, is *H. rosrata*.

Hyacinth

Around 30 species, named after Hyacinthus, lover of the god Apollo. When Hyacinthus was accidentally killed, hyacinths were said to spring from his blood. As a cut flower, it brings bold definition and a glorious scent to any arrangement.

Tulip

A very early variety of plant, the tulip was first brought to Europe from Constantinople in 1562. Now, almost 4,000 horticultural varieties have been developed. With its wide range of colours – almost every shade except true blue – and forms, it is one of the most popular flowers.

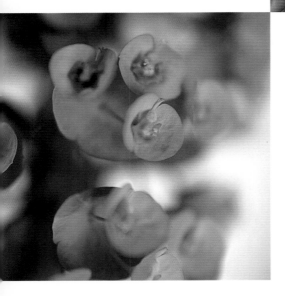

Spurge

This is another green flower to add a touch of the vividly unexpected to an arrangement. To my mind, the best variety is *Euphorbia characias* subsp. *wulfenii*, a perennial with bluish-green leaves and nodding flowers. *E. polychroma* comes a close second.

Gladiolus

A genus of over 150 species that flower in late summer and were fashionable about 30 years ago. I feel their time has come again. Nothing beats a mass of single-colour gladioli stems in a vase. They last well as cut flowers too.

Lilac

Most common in white or lilac colour, lilac usually has a lovely subtle fragrance. Unfortunately, it does not last long once cut, and many people are wary of having it indoors as it is sometimes thought to bring bad luck.

Guelder rose

A must for any flower-lover's garden, this is a most wonderful shrub. As its acid-green flowers grow, they develop into puffy, creamy-white balls. In autumn the shrub becomes a mass of red berries and terrific rich, vibrant red foliage.

Tuberose

Tuberoses have the most amazing creamy-white flowers, often tinged with pink, and a heavy, rich scent. They grow only in warm climates, so are often imported and therefore expensive to buy and, unfortunately, do not last well when cut. But they are worth it.

Guelder rose

Although the flowers of the guelder rose look good with almost anything, they are especially spectacular combined with purple and orange.

Aspidistra

Very popular as a house plant in the nineteenth century but I like to use it for its bold architectural foliage, folded around the edge of a hand-tied bouquet, or submerged in water in a clear glass vase. It lasts extremely well.

Dogwood

A shrub whose bare winter stems have many uses. I like the red *Cornus alba* at Christmas, mixed with other winter foliage and wrapped around containers, or for staking amaryllis. I also wrap the pale greenish-yellow *C. stolonifera* 'Flaviramea' around the stems of dried-flower trees.

Flowering eucalyptus

Very useful Australian foliage. I use shorter lengths of flowering eucalyptus (*E. perriniana*) in hand-tied bouquets, or as a base for table decorations. Longer stems are ideal in large urns. Other varieties are useful too – the large round leaves of *E. gunnii*, and feathery *E. parvifolia*.

Garrya elliptica

Another great garden shrub suitable for a south- or west-facing wall. In early winter It bears amazing silver-green catkins that add an air of mystery and sense of movement to any composition, whether it be an arrangement or a hand-tied bouquet.

tomorrow's classics

Horsetail

A foliage with many uses. Dress up a container with stems of horsetail glued to the outside. Submerge it in water in a glass vase so that the fascinating stems are magnified. Split it and use it to cover canes that support a flowering orchid.

Brachyglottis 'Sunshine'

This silvery-grey evergreen has got to be one of my all-time favourites, both in the garden and for flower arranging. It adds an English country feel to whatever you mix it with, and looks especially good in all-white compositions.

Magnolia grandiflora

A real garden favourite of mine. Beautiful just as it is, or grown as a large-leafed topiary tree, or against a wall. Its glossy evergreen leaves have a wonderful textured suede underside. Dried, they can be used to make sculptured trees. A great base foliage.

Photinia 'Red Robin'

Another excellent garden shrub whose new spring leaves are a beautiful bronze-red colour. It makes a stunningly opulent composition with other reds and purples. I still find it very useful as a base foliage once the foliage has matured and turned a rich green.

Bear grass

This native of Texas and the Mexican highlands is useful for its delicate, loose habit. I like to use it in hand-tied bouquets, especially wedding bouquets. It also works well in more graphic arrangements.

...foliage

Fan palm

Palm leaves are a must for a tropical
arrangement, even as an edging for a
tropical hand-tied bouquet. They are great,
too, laid flat on a table as a base for a
display of tropical fruit. They will dry
quickly if you leave them out of water. Try
them sprayed gold for Christmas.

Galax

This useful plant from eastern North
America has evergreen leaves that often
turn bronze in winter. They can last up to
three weeks in water. I like to use them as
an edging to a small hand-tied bouquet, and
I sometimes wrap them round glass night-
lights for an extra decorative touch.

Feathered papyrus

A lush green grass-like foliage with a
tropical-marsh quality. For a tropical foliage
arrangement, I mix it with anthurium leaves,
fan palm and clumps of horsetail. The
stems, all cut to the same length and tied
together, can make an unusual ball shape
like an oriental-style topiary.

Anthurium

These very distinctive heart-shaped, dark
green glossy leaves last well in water. I love
to use them as a bold defining collar around
the edge of a vase. Otherwise, a single leaf
looks great with a stem of, say, amaryllis – a
striking flower that can hold its own.

Cycas palm

This glossy dark green leaf has a very strong character. Only flowers of similar strength can stand up to it. I love combining it with bold white flowers such as amaryllis, or 'Casa Blanca' lilies.

Variegated pittosporum

Pittosporums are great garden shrubs but, as they are slow-growing, you are unlikely to want to cut them. Commercially grown large- or small-leafed variegated varieties are available instead. They go with most colour palettes, and their variegation will add sparkle to any arrangement.

Papyrus

This amazing plant bears an enormous profusion of grass-like tufts from its lush green fibrous stem. Added to any arrangement , it brings a strong sense of structure. On its own, with its tufts trimmed to the same length, it is unbeatable.

Ming fern

This foliage has a strongly oriental character which suits the company of other oriental plants. For a minimalist arrangement, use it with a few stems of cymbidium or phalaenopsis orchids. The result will be simple but stylish.

Swiss cheese plant

One of the most distinctive leaf forms I have ever used. Its glossy green, deeply cut contours are effective as an edging to an arrangement or – my favourite – under water in a clear glass vase to help disguise the stems of other flowers.

x *Vuylstekeara* cambria orchid
With its exotic, complex flower, this orchid
can range from white to dark burgundy.
Planted in a simple wooden container
topped with bark chippings, it adds a dose
of magically intense colour, especially in a
richly decorated dark-panelled room.

Paphiopedilum orchid
My favourite of these orchids is
P. x 'Maudiae', the lovely green-and-white
variety shown here. The flower itself
reminds me of a bumble bee – the very
insect it is designed to attract for polination.

Hyacinth
One of the treats of including hyacinth
bulbs in an arrangement is that you can
watch them grow. Individual white
hyacinths in creamware pots, each with a
plant label giving the guest's name, look
stunning for a wedding-party table setting.

Phalaenoposis orchid
A classic of the orchid world. Its arching
stems with – usually – white flowers look
best just on their own. It also comes in hot
pink and cream. Take care when planting
into your own container, as it doesn't like its
roots being disturbed.

tomorrow's classics

Dendrobium orchid

This white dendrobium orchid – the orchid most commonly sold as a plant – is my favourite. Other stunners are 'Madame Pompadour' – a strking purple – and 'James Storey' – a dark orange-red, often used with autumn foliage and winter evergreens.

Amaryllis

A stately, architectural bulb to grow yourself and brighten up the winter. At Christmas I love to see red ones in dark wooden bowls or baskets. White looks good in galvanised or creamware pots, topped with grey lichen.

Jasmine

Jasmine is a classic plant that looks best on its own, for instance on a coffee table. For a classic setting I might use it in a creamware pot supported by twigs of silver birch. For a contemporary location, simply spray the twigs with silver paint.

Ivy topiary

Ivy can be trained along wires to form different shapes – a solid ball, a hollow globe, or even an animal shape. Use small-leafed varieties, preferably plain green and not variegated. It can be trained quite quickly – one season should give your shape – but watch out for insects.

'Tête-à-tête' narcissus

With its not-too-large blooms and long flowering period, this is one of the most commonly grown narcissi. I love to plant a mass of them in a glass container lined with gravel and topped with lush green bun moss. Use birch twigs if they need staking.

...plants

marmalade skies

I love the yellows. They range from pale, delicate narcissi to bright gold forsythia, and from orange gourds and pumpkins to rusty lilies. Chinese witch hazel is one of my favourite plants, with its amazing fragrance and flowers like crinkled ribbon. The bonus is its wonderful golden-yellow leaves in autumn. Cornelian cherry is another favourite with small clusters of spiky yellow flowers on its bare winter branches, while in summer, no matter where I am, the sight of sunflower fields always reminds me of Umbria in Italy.

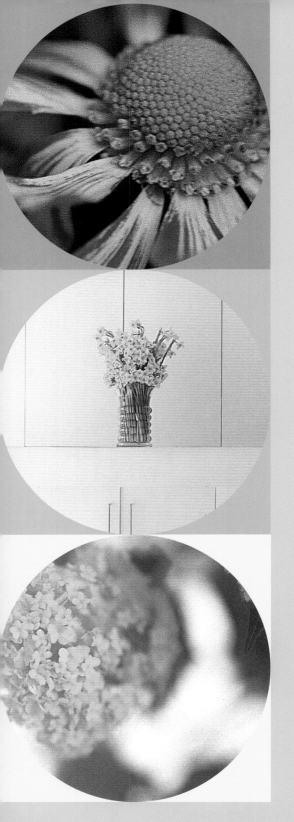

Left, from top
Sunny-faced rudbeckias, bright
yellow narcissi and the
greenish-yellow of the guelder
rose show how tones of yellow
make a splash whatever the
time of year.

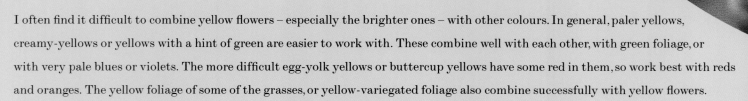

I often find it difficult to combine yellow flowers – especially the brighter ones – with other colours. In general, paler yellows, creamy-yellows or yellows with a hint of green are easier to work with. These combine well with each other, with green foliage, or with very pale blues or violets. The more difficult egg-yolk yellows or buttercup yellows have some red in them, so work best with reds and oranges. The yellow foliage of some of the grasses, or yellow-variegated foliage also combine successfully with yellow flowers.

Solid yellow-white gerbera contrast with delicate sprays of lady's mantle. The colours of the variegated pittosporum pull all the yellows together. Lady's mantle, fresh or dried, is invaluable.

the freshness of spring

LEFT AND BELOW

For this arrangement, I used a medium-weave rectangular basket lined with a plastic bowl filled with chicken wire. First I made a base of berried ivy, and of forsythia, hazel and alder catkins. Then I threaded through long stems of white Christmas roses. Displayed in this basket, the flowers look as if they have just been picked from the garden.

BELOW

To make the smaller arrangement I put in a row of forsythia, all cut to the same height, then threaded the Christmas roses through. I especially love seeing the stems of the flowers through the frosted Perspex.

Here, I wanted to show what can be done using the same flowers – forsythia and Christmas roses – but in different ways. Christmas roses always remind me of my mother as she is a great collector of plants and grows them in her garden. They are truly wonderful, with their clusters of nodding heads on long stems bringing a breath of life to the garden during the cold winter months. As well as white, Christmas roses also come in a pale pink, burgundy, shades of green and even a yellow, so they are very versatile plants for flower arrangers. The main arrangement here is in traditional country-house style, but I have given it an interesting twist by putting this classic in modern surroundings. The other arrangement, in a flat, narrow vase made of frosted Perspex and without the catkins, has a very much more contemporary feel to it.

This arrangement happened more by accident than by design. When I bought the dried roses I carried them home in the wooden crate. It was the first container I laid my hands on. Then I simply rearranged the roses slightly. The result is unexpectedly successful.

This is another example of what can be done using the same material but in different ways. During the winter months, when the crate is not filled with sunflower plants (see page 55), I use it to show off several bunches of dried yellow roses. I have simply laid them in the crate in a casual, country manner. For a classic feel, pairs of creamware pots, like those above and opposite, look good placed on a mantelpiece, a dressing table or, as here, on an attractive old side table. The lamp adds a lovely finishing touch, casting its warm glow on the objects against the yellow wall. Pots like these also work very well in a contemporary location, say as a pair offset on a glass-topped coffee table, or on Perspex side tables with lamps, on each side of a bed.

dried yellow roses

It is easy to fill creamware pots with dried roses like this. Just fill your pot with a round ball of florist's foam, leaving a third of the foam above the rim, then simply push the rose heads in, starting with the row closest to the rim. Continue row by row until you reach the centre.

These golden shower orchids always remind me of miniature yellow butterflies, so delicate, yet so vibrant when the sun shines through them. Here I have used them in a bowl surrounded by my favourite honeycomb candles. The rich texture and colour of the candles makes an interesting and original combination with the copper wire wrapped around them. To form the support that holds the candles, cut a piece of chicken wire deep enough to conceal the bowl and long enough to wrap around it several times. Attach it to the bowl with criss-cross wire. To position the candles, push a length of wire through each, twist its ends together, and use the twisted ends to wire the candles to the chicken-wire collar. The copper wire around the outside adds extra support and is a nice design detail, while the clusters of three small candles make a lovely finishing touch. With some care, orchids are long-lasting. Don't overwater as they do not like to be sitting in moisture. Also, try and keep them out of direct sunlight. As the old flowers fade, new ones develop. If you are lucky, you might manage to persuade this variety of orchid to flower again the following year.

golden shower orchids

1

Make a chicken-wire collar and fix it around the bowl. Wire in the candles, turning them upside down so the wicks do not show and they cannot be lit.

2

Wrap copper wire around the outside of the candles, then add groups of three small candles using more copper wire.

3

Pot the orchids into the bowl using special orchid compost. I used three plants and left some of their roots showing to add to the effect.

4

Add natural canes to support the orchids and for colour co-ordination. Tie the stems to them with small pieces of copper wire.

5

Level off the compost then dress it with grains of wheat. Their colour links with that of the candles and the orchids. You can use moss or lichen instead.

The table is of frosted glass with a clear glass centre, and I used frosted and clear glassware at the place settings to echo this. The frosted glass picks up the colour of the white narcissi while the golden pine floorboards, seen through the centre of the table, complement the yellow ones.

This test-tube snake is one of my favourite vases. It consists of a metal frame holding clear glass test tubes, and can be bent to the shape you want. I have also used it to hold white nerines and papyrus (see page 134). Here, I have made the vase into a circle and placed it as a centrepiece on a circular dining table. The arrangement itself is very simple – nothing more than alternating clusters of 'Paper White' and 'Soleil d'Or' narcissi. As a final touch, I have positioned clear glass night-lights within the circle made by the vase. The light reflects through the water and stems and across the table in a particularly magical way.

Narcissi come in many guises, ranging from delicate single white flowers through creamy doubles and the cyclamen-type with reflexed petals to bright yellow trumpets. They are brilliant either as cut flowers or in the garden, and if you grow them indoors you can plant them in the garden afterwards to flower again the following year. Among my favourites are 'Paper White' narcissi, with their amazing fragrance and glistening white flowers, and 'Bridal Crown', whose cream and orange semi-double flowers again have a beautiful scent and last well as cut flowers.

narcissi

The linear quality of this minimalist white interior lends itself to the simple, clear glass vase and the succulent, chunky stems of the narcissi. I packed in as many stems as possible to produce a substantial, compact head of flowers. As a focal point at the end of a limestone walkway, the arrangement looks as if it is floating above the cupboards.

The centre of the arrangement is
made from a base of variegated
pittosporum and lady's mantle.
The last step is to add clusters
of bright yellow and pale green
mini gerberas.

lemon basket

This arrangement makes me think of a game of tennis on a summer afternoon. I'm longing for a

glass of home-made lemonade and a slice of luscious lemon cake. I can't think of anything more

perfect. The arrangement is simple to make, even if it doesn't look it. Start with a chicken-wire

collar around a plastic bowl. Make it in the same way as the collar for the golden shower orchids

(see page 44). Wire up the lemons by sticking a length of medium wire through the centre of each

and twisting the ends of the wire together, then wire a lower row of lemons to the collar, followed

by an upper one. Fill the plastic bowl with crumpled chicken wire, add the water, and finally

position the flowers and foliage.

This audacious arrangement of yellow and orange rose heads was designed to make a stunning impact on a console table in a formal hallway. It certainly adds a touch of the unexpected with its sizzling colours and rough wood container. I could also see a tray of roses like this one gracing the centre of a large dining table, where its low lines would not impede dinner-table conversation. If you are handy, you can easily make a container like mine from rough wood planks and some thick rope. When not being used for roses, it would look equally appealing filled with rows of red and green apples, or with walnuts and chestnuts.

Roses are expensive to buy, and I use a large quantity of them here – in fact over a hundred 'Pareo' and 'Golden Gates' – so this really is an arrangement for a special occasion. You will want the roses to last as long as possible, so you should give them a good long drink of water before you arrange them. Also, you should make sure the wooden tray is well lined with heavy polythene to prevent water from leaking out.

rows of roses

1

Carefully line a wooden tray with heavy polythene, making sure the polythene comes well up the sides of the tray.

2

Fill the tray with blocks of florist's foam that have been soaked in a bucket of water for several hours.

3

Remove any foliage and trim the stems of the roses at an angle. Arrange the first row of rose heads along the side of the tray.

4

Add more rose heads until one

block of colour is complete.

5

Continue adding roses,

alternating the blocks of colour,

until the tray is full.

foxtail lilies

The sunshine-yellow of the wall is complemented by the yellow foxtail lilies, and the handrail by the bulrushes and millet grass. The base of green and yellow variegated euonymus gives the arrangement a lift, while the foxtail lilies with their very solid, rather heavy stems add a relaxed feel.

LEFT

One of the things I love about this mixture of flowers is their similarity of shape and form. They are all predominantly spiky but have different textures. The compact density of the millet grass reflects that of the bulrushes. The long stems of foxtail lilies are similar in shape, but have a looser habit. The air between each flower gives them a light and elegant feel.

This striking arrangement shows the beautiful harmonies that can be created using the full range of yellows, from pale, greenish-yellow to dark rusty oranges. It was when I was decorating a friend's house for a party that I noticed this spot on the landing. It needed a large and fairly classical arrangement, so I filled a great black cast-iron urn with a mass of late-summer flowers. I would have preferred to arrange the flowers in water but, because the bowl of the urn was too small for a sufficiently large water-holding container, I had to arrange them in wet florist's foam which is not quite so satisfactory. Using quality flowers like these, you will want the arrangement to last as long as possible, so keep the florist's foam wet by topping up the water daily. If you pick off the lower flowers of the foxtail lilies as they fade they can last two weeks or more.

For a late-summer arrangement, line a crate with polythene and plant it with yellow sunflowers. This is the perfect size to place in the middle of a buffet table for a summer party, to give the table some height.

If I had used roses with bigger heads to decorate this hat, I would only have used three but, whatever the size, my rule of thumb is to always use clusters of flowers in odd numbers – threes, fives, sevens, and so on.

spirit of summer

The full, open heads of roses and the happy, smiling faces of sunflowers both capture the spirit of summer. The crate that in winter was filled with dried yellow roses (see page 42), is now planted with yellow sunflowers. The woven hat, looking almost like a basket of thin cane, was crying out for a trimming of summer grasses and roses. First I made a strip of plaited grass which I fixed around the crown like a hatband. Then I picked a simple bunch of meadow grass from the hedgerow, folded the end of the bunch back on itself, and fixed it with a thick wire to the plaited grass band. You could use bear grass if meadow grass is not available. Finally, I wired five coffee-coloured 'Safari' roses onto the grass band with some more stems of meadow grass.

Tulips make brilliant cut flowers. From the minute you buy them they keep on changing their form and character. You can watch them develop from tight buds into open blooms, and then fade – the process is fascinating. Whether you indulge in huge bunches of field-grown varieties or whether you yearn for the simplicity of a single 'Black Parrot' tulip, there truly are tulips for every style and mood. They are not renowned for their scent, but for their variety of different shapes. There are feathered Parrot tulips, pointed Lily-flowered tulips, and the traditional turban style. As they are available most of the year, they are a boon for flower arrangers.

tulips

BELOW
The wonderful thing about tulips is that they can be placed casually in a simple glass vase like this and left to do their own thing. They look great.

RIGHT
What could be simpler than a row of glass bottles, each holding just one double tulip? They will make a great display on a kitchen windowsill or on a narrow table-top.

I remember tulips well from my student days at the Royal Horticultural Society gardens at Wisley in Surrey, so I have a special fondness for them. We used to use them as spring bedding plants – yellow 'Bellona' early single tulips with a soft haze of pale blue forget-me-nots as an underplanting for the roses in the formal rose garden. Nowadays I find the long-stemmed French varieties, single or double and in a wonderful range of colours, very exciting. I also love miniature tulips which can be grown successfully in pots and brought indoors.

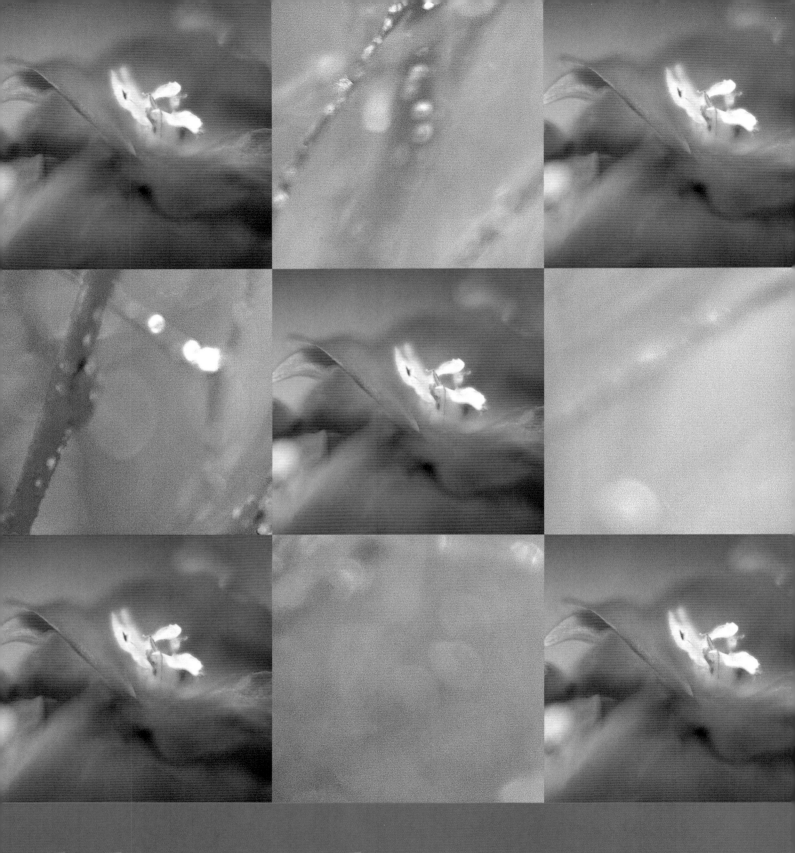

blue velvet

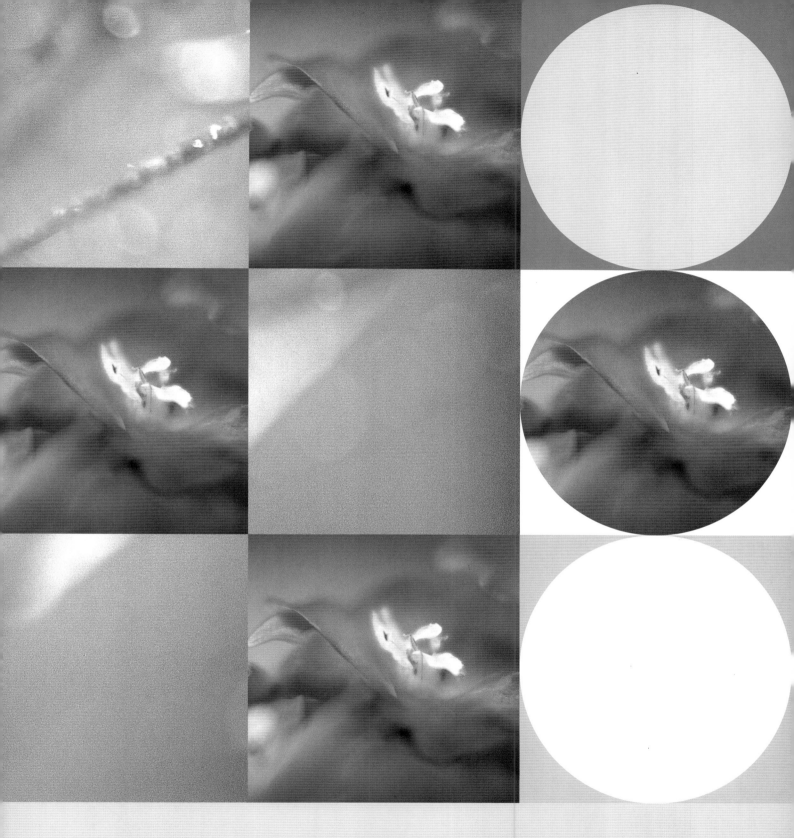

Blue reminds me of spring. I love it when the woods near my home are covered in hazy drifts of bluebells, like a dream-like patchwork quilt. Blue also makes me think of the sea, from soft grey-blue under a winter sky to clear green-blue in the sunlight. I only have to put together a bunch of sea holly with driftwood and pebbles to conjure up an image of a sun-bleached seaside garden. Blue is also for relaxation, mystery and coolness. If I add blue flowers to a mixed arrangement, they lend it an air of subtlety and calm.

LEFT, FROM TOP
Nature looks so perfect dressed in blue. It never ceases to amaze me that glistening globe thistles can grow to such a wonderful shape, or that blues can come as delicate as this misty gladiolus flower. The blue-sprayed silver birch twigs look positively ethereal with their dusting of silver.

Blues come in many guises. Soft blues are traditional for a new-born baby boy, but dark blues send a more powerful message. Deep blue hyacinths and delphiniums resonate alongside purple lisianthus, but add white flowers such as tulips or snapdragons for a crisp, nautical effect. I love blues in the garden, too, especially in combination with silver-grey foliage. Lavender, with its beautiful flower and foliage colour and its heavenly scent, has it all, while my favourite blue climbing plant is wisteria.

Grape hyacinths are among my favourite spring bulbs. They look stunning massed together, whether in the garden or in a vase. This vase is perfect for them. Its sexy curves echo the curves of the tiny, individual, bell-like flowers.

For this classic look, put a mass of delphiniums together. Place the tallest stems — all cut to the same length — first, then support them with a few shorter ones at the front.

In general, garden-grown
delphiniums shed their petals
indoors sooner than the
commercially cultivated ones,
but I find that the dark blue
D. (Belladonna Group) 'Blue
Bees', the cream *D.* (Belladonna
Group) 'Casa Blanca', and the
white Pacific Giant hybrids
shown here all last extremely
well as cut flowers.

delphiniums

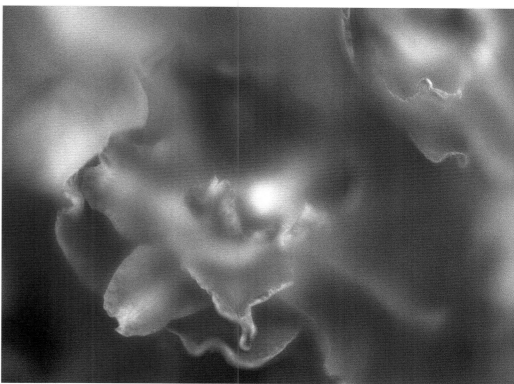

Traditionally a cottage-garden plant, delphiniums are flowers I love to grow in a herbaceous
border. They add such drama. They are the only flowers I know that have such strongly defined
spires in the blue colour range. They can grow very tall and so need staking. Sometimes I use
these very long stems to add stateliness to an arrangement, but the smaller-flowered
commercially cultivated varieties are wonderful too. Some of the colours have a lustre to them
which gives them an almost crystalline translucency. Putting all the shades together like this
makes them look almost unreal. They certainly don't need any more adornment.

The violets stand in simple terracotta pots. The saucers have been painted silver, and the pots a lilac colour. This shade of lilac works well with the silver and gives the whole arrangement an easy-to-live-with, contemporary feel. I have arranged the pots in three rows of three, like a living sculpture.

The violet, with its strong, vibrant jewel-like depth of colour, its contrasting dark green veined leaves and its heady scent, is a wonderfully old-fashioned flower. It is not the easiest flower to use as it has a short stem and wilts very quickly. I am not sure if that is the origin of the name 'shrinking violet'. If you do decide to use violets, be sure to re-cut their stems and place the flowers in water immediately. If you can't find cut violets, you can achieve the same look by using purple African violet plants which would last a lot longer. This composition would also work well with single blue hyacinth bulbs or with acid-green mind-your-own-business.

violets

A glass liner inside each pot
holds the water and three
bunches of violets edged with
their leaves.

It's best to make the tree when the branches have no leaves on them. At that stage they are pliable, but not so soft that they cannot take any weight. Kept out of strong sunlight, the thistles will hold their natural blue colour for many years. To stop the tree from getting dusty, periodically wave a hairdrier, on a cold setting, over it. The tree smells wonderful sprinkled with lavender oil.

For a cloud tree, you need stems of contorted hazel or willow in a pot filled with quick-setting plaster. As the plaster dries, it may crack the pot so use a plastic one that will fit into an outer pot. Attach clumps of chicken wire to the stems, fill the chicken wire with moss, then wire up the individual thistle heads and fix them to the moss, starting with the lowest row of each cloud. To disguise the mechanics, glue grey lichen to the underside of each cloud. Make an odd number of clouds, arranging them with the largest at the bottom of the tree and the smallest at the top.

This arrangement of contorted willow or hazel with globe thistles looks like soft clouds caught up in the branches of a tree. It was inspired by the modern, asymmetrical look of the fireplace. It's more common to use an evenly spaced pair of containers on a mantelpiece, but because of the way the wall behind was painted I felt the left-hand side of the scheme needed emphasising to adjust the balance. I also thought that the strictness of the painted wall and fireplace would look better with the soft lines of a cloud tree than if I had used a more formal topiary tree.

blue cloud tree

The shape of this tree reminds
me of the cedar of Lebanon,
which grows in many old,
established gardens.

Christmas is a time when people like to decorate their front doors with a wreath to welcome their guests. Here, I have taken the traditional Christmas wreath, but have given it a new slant by using shades of blue instead of the usual green, red and gold. The wreath is not as difficult as it looks. I started with a circle of wire covered with moss, then attached a base of blue spruce, arranged so that its tips all followed the line of the circle. Next, I added criss-cross clusters of lavender, all cut to the same length and tied with raffia. Last to go in were the groups of white gourds, and bunches of eucalyptus pods. A wreath like this should last for around four weeks.

I love using eucalyptus pods, not only because of their fascinating shape, but also because of their colour – they look as if they have been limewashed. They are, in fact, flowers whose petals fuse together as they mature. When the top of the pod falls off, the stamens appear. These have that familiar eucalyptus aroma.

gourd wreath

This conservatory seemed to me to be the perfect location for a tower of glass cones supported in a metal frame and planted with blue hyacinths. The arrangement works well with the surrounding hard materials – the alloy frame and the corrugated metal walls of the conservatory – while the blue of the hyacinths complements the glass walls. The fact that the hyacinths are growing softens the whole effect. I love the reflection of it all in the mirror, and couldn't wait to get the finished tower into position. An alternative to planting the hyacinths in a tower like this would be simply to plant them in a deep glass dish. That would look stunningly cosmopolitan sitting on a glass coffee or dining table.

towering hyacinths

1

Supporting the cone in a deep container, line it with grey lichen. Place some drainage material such as gravel or clay granules in the bottom.

2

Select an odd number of forced hyacinth bulbs. They should all be at the same stage of development.

3

Plant the hyacinths, adding plenty of compost around their roots, then water well and top off with more grey lichen.

sea holly & roses

FAR LEFT AND LEFT
The fleshy round heads of the
roses and sea holly contrast
sharply with the sea holly's
jagged, silvery bracts and with
the fine stems of the
eucalyptus. The colour
contrasts double the effect of
the contrasts of shape.

I love having a neutral background to which I can add an element of surprise in the form of
unexpected colour. In this setting, I started with a subtle palette of tones – cream, white and beige.
For contrast, I have chosen a translucent blue vase. Placed on a glass side table in a window, the vase
is backlit, revealing the lovely outline of the stems of the flowers and foliage. The base of this
arrangement is flowering eucalyptus and *Brachyglottis* 'Sunshine'. Then I added the lush stems of
sea holly, with its sea-anemone-type flowers in silver-blue. Next I wove in some stems of purple
lisianthus with its cup-shaped flowers, and finally I added orange 'Pareo' roses. The zingy
combination of orange with purple is great, adding a dose of vitality to the arrangement.

The driftwood is a subtle silver-grey which complements beautifully the blue of the anemones. It also provides a colour and shape link with the chrome legs of the table. The driftwood and the pebbles are magnified by the water which adds a further dimension to this unusual arrangement.

This design was created for a fiftieth birthday party, for someone who is passionate about fishing. So what could be better, I thought, than to include fish in the table decoration? With this in mind, I placed a goldfish in its bowl in a circular dish filled with wet florist's foam, and studded the foam with rings of blue anemones, starting at the outer edge and finishing as close as I could to the goldfish bowl. The anemones make the water look blue and contrast beautifully with the colour of the fish. For extra interest, I put some pebbles in the bottom of the bowl and included two pieces of driftwood, to introduce the idea of the water's link with the land.

anemones & driftwood

lined-up blues

To underscore the geometry of this arrangement, I spent some time cutting all the stems of lavender to the same length. This gives the arrangement a flat, table-top effect which works well with the straight-sided metal pots.

The row of vases reflects the strict design of the balcony, while the cornflowers give a relaxed, rural feel. They almost look as if they are growing. Seeing their stems through the frosted glass reminds me of hazy summer skies.

Depending on what you put in them, rows of matching pots or vases can suit modern or traditional locations. Lavender is usually associated with traditional country interiors. A mass of it stuffed into an old terracotta pot looks as if it has just been collected from the garden. That same concept, but approached in a contemporary way, can work in a modern setting too. For a classic interior that has been modernised, my choice was three square matching galvanised metal pots placed in a row and crammed with cut lavender. These pots would also look superb filled with mind-your-own-business plants. These are available in acid-green, lime-green, variegated gold and plain green varieties, offering a choice for any colour scheme.

To complement my old French wrought-iron balcony, I opted for the simplicity of a row of frosted glass vases filled with blue cornflowers. I arranged the flowers very loosely and informally. I like the mix of the modern, crisp, frosted glass with the old, characterful balcony. This arrangement would also be successful using Iceland poppies. With their loose habit and long stems, they are rather similar to the cornflowers.

A galvanised dustbin and co-ordinating colours give a contemporary twist to a traditional Christmas tree. My preference is for white lights on any Christmas tree, but especially on this one where white complements the silver of the dustbin and the blue of the spray-painted branches. Stabilise the dustbin by filling it with sand and, if there are to be young children around, you might consider wiring the lower branches of the tree to the dustbin handles as an extra safety precaution. Choose a spruce or fir tree, if possible with non-dropping needles, and always use a mask and follow the manufacturer's instructions when you are applying the spray paint. When you arrange the lights in the tree, loop them along the length of the branches rather than round and round the tree. This distributes them more evenly and looks more natural. Check if the lights are well positioned by half-closing your eyes. The lights will seem to sparkle more, making it easier to judge the effect.

christmas tree

1

Remove the bulbs from the
Christmas tree lights and spray
the flex silver. Separate the
branches of the tree using the
flat of your hand.

2

Spray the branches with matte,
pale blue paint, spraying up and
down for even coverage.

3

Replace the light bulbs and arrange the lights on the tree along the length of the branches.

4

Wire the blue baubles onto the branches, taking care that they are evenly spaced.

These purplish-mauve gladioli are an astonishingly beautiful colour. They really leap out at you. In this composition, the glass shapes edging the mirror reflect the shape of the individual gladiolius flowers.

gladioli

Thanks to the minimalist movement in interior design, gladioli are staging a come-back. With their tall stems and strong, bold flowers in colours ranging from white, blue, yellow, red, burgundy and pink to an amazing green – 'Green Woodpecker' – they are the flowers to watch out for. They are also very versatile, and equally effective in an industrial-looking vase of metal rods lined with blown glass or cut down and placed in small pots so that the emphasis is on the beauty of their individual flowers. They also last very well. With a long-stemmed arrangement, you can take off the lower flowers as they fade. This encourages the buds to open.

Here I underline the architectural quality of the gladioli by using them in a concrete block installation on the floor. I have set a square metal vase in one cavity of the block, filling it with a mass of red gladioli. In the other, I have placed a beaker of water with a pair of rolled-up dark green *Farfugium japonicum* leaves.

RIGHT, INSET
Laid along a shallow dish, single gladiolus flowers can make a very quick and simple table centrepiece. As an alternative, they would look great floating in water in a glass bowl.

strawberry fields

As bright, strong colours take over in popularity from pastel shades, red has to be one of my favourite colours. It is linked with festivity and romance. Different tones of red can be found in many exciting flowers, in all the seasons and across the full spectrum. You only have to think of dark red roses, magenta monarda, scarlet dahlias or pale pink peonies. I quite often like to put shades of red together or, alternatively, to add another strong colour such as purple which makes for a very special and intense combination.

LEFT, FROM TOP
A pale pink gerbera, its centre fringed with tiny darker petals, a mid-pink flowering prunus, and a cluster of fringed red and white Parrot tulips surrounded by suede-effect *Magnolia grandiflora* leaves show something of the range of red tones that nature can produce.

Red is a colour I use throughout the year. It is festive at Christmas and is the obvious choice for Valentine's Day. At the height of summer, I incorporate in my arrangements the lush soft fruits that are in season, while in autumn reddish foliage is a must. Reds merge into purples with *Rosa glauca*, syn. *R. rubrifolia*, with the plum-red foliage of the smoke tree, and with the burgundy berries of hypericum. Reds become almost black with the flowers of chocolate cosmos, which actually smell of chocolate.

I love the gradation of colour in this pink arum lily, from the almost burgundy tips of its petals to its pale pink veined centre. Arums come in other bright colours – burnt orange and yellow, for instance – but the classic colour is white.

This modern, blue wire-mesh container gives the normally traditional peony a completely different, contemporary flavour. Here I have placed an odd number of mid-pink peonies – some of them double-flowering – around the rim of the container, and have filled in with dark red, scented blooms.

Peonies are great as cut flowers and look equally effective in a contemporary or traditional arrangement. Available in many varieties and a wonderful range of colours, some are even scented which is an added bonus. Most have the characteristic 'over the top' size of bloom – I have seen some with heads as large as 25cm/10in across. Varieties that I love to grow for cutting include some cultivars of *Paeonia lactiflora* – the clear, pale pink 'Sarah Bernhardt', the dark red 'Karl Rosenfield' and the white, slightly blushed with pink 'Duchesse de Nemours'. Peonies can be dried rather easily, but this must be done quickly so that they will not drop their petals. Just hang them upside down in a very warm place for a couple of weeks. Once dried, they look terrific as an edging for a basket of pot-pourri.

peonies

This Dutch still-life-style
arrangement of peonies would
suit a country interior. I
especially love the trailing
scented jasmine. For evening,
the arrangement could be
enhanced with drifts of red
plums, cherries and
strawberries around the base,
and red glass night-lights.

ABOVE
Dried peonies also look great.
Fill a terracotta pot with florist's
foam and top it with moss, then
place the peonies as you would
fresh ones, but closer together.
Because they shrink when
dried, you will need almost
twice as many blooms as for
the arrangement on the left.

Following the principle of always using odd numbers, I have hung three clear glass test tubes from a stair rail and have put a stem of ornamental cabbage in each. What I love about using test tubes is the way they highlight the bold colour of whatever they contain – in this case, the cut stems of the cabbages.

In the future, I am sure we shall be using more industrial-looking containers as flower holders. They really seem to capture the pared-down, industrial spirit of our age, but their effect is softened by wonderful blooms. These two arrangements show how much can be achieved simply by lining up a number of beautiful, individual specimens in a row. For the first, I used ornamental cabbages. They are among my favourite plants. I like white ones best of all, but they also come in green, as well as in the pink I have used here. Whenever I plan a kitchen garden, I always add a few of these plants for fun. They look terrific in containers too. In the other arrangement I have used four elegant, sinuous pink arum lilies. Like the cabbages, they look stunning all in a row.

sinuous shapes

BELOW
The clean lines of this metal-framed test-tube holder and the clarity of its glass tubes make a marvellous container for single-stem specimens such as these wonderful pink arum lilies. Arranged in this way, the individual beauty of each flower becomes part of a strong whole.

Red is such a strong colour that it often needs nothing more than the green of its foliage to set it off. These arrangements demonstrate that point to perfection. The terracotta pot would make a wonderful centrepiece for an autumn dinner party, or would look stunning placed on a side table under a lamp to bring out the richness of its colours. The basket of red cyclamen makes a truly eye-catching gift and would provide more long-lasting pleasure than a bouquet of flowers. This miniature red cyclamen is slightly scented and, as long as you pick off any dead flowers, will last for many weeks. As a complete contrast, the minimalist arrangement of burgundy ranunculus would be ideal for a crisp, modern table setting. Ranunculus flowers are so perfect you might almost think they were made from tissue paper.

LEFT
This arrangement consists of berried ivy, cotoneaster berries, hypericum, poke weed, ornamental crab apple, burgundy snapdragons, red nerines and clusters of 'Vicky Brown' roses. I have also used a red spray rose – 'Tamango' – and spiky stems of *Pavonia* x *gledhillii* pods to give the arrangement some strength.

BELOW
Here I garlanded a basket with long, twining stems of honeysuckle to add interesting texture and to make the basket look less man-made. Make sure you line the basket well with double-thickness polythene to prevent water leaking out.

fire and ice

The black-lacquered tray of
champagne glasses
filled with raffia-tied burgundy
ranunculus shows that it is not
flowers alone that make for a
successful arrangement.

hand-tied roses

No matter what the occasion – a special celebration, a thank you, or simply a romantic gesture – a bunch of roses always makes a welcome present. There are so many beautiful varieties around now, but my favourites are 'Nicole' – raspberry with a whitish undercolour, 'Vicky Brown' – reddish-brown, with an undercolour like tan suede, and the 'Black Magic' shown here – a stunning velvety dark red. It's terribly easy to make a hand-tied bouquet like this one. If you first make the basic shape with the foliage, the rest will fall into place. Here I have used five pieces of berried ivy, with their lower leaves removed. Then I added twelve long-stemmed roses – lower leaves and thorns removed and stems cut at an angle – placing them slightly higher than the foliage in the centre, and slightly deeper around the edges to produce a gentle mound. If roses are too traditional for your taste, then any round-headed flowers would do. Anemones or gerberas would give a more contemporary look.

1

Holding the ivy in one hand, arrange it into a bouquet.

2

Thread the roses through, spacing them equally throughout and trying to maintain a slightly rounded shape to the bouquet.

3

Using a piece of raffia, tie the bouquet together quite high up the stems, then trim the stems all to the same length.

4

Fold several layers of white tissue paper so that they form two points.

5

Wrap the tissue paper around the bouquet, then repeat with a second layer of paper.

6

Wrap in clear cellophane, then tie with a bow made of strands of raffia. Finish by trimming the ends of the raffia bow.

With a lovely summer's evening and a willow-tree backdrop that was the very willow of Kenneth Grahame's *The Wind in the Willows*, a special table setting was called for. The burgundy velvet tablecloth is smothered with a profusion of riches – purple sage, mint, hyssop, thyme, flat-leafed parsley and spikes of purple heuchera, all brimming out of old terracotta pots. More pots are filled with heads of 'Only Love' roses, with the spray red rose 'Domingo', with chocolate cosmos and with stems of fruiting blackberry.

wind in the willows

Drifts of fruit laid on dark green leaves to enhance their colour, together with clusters of red glass night-lights, complement the herbs and flowers. At each place setting is a potted herb, its plant label serving as a place card. Sprigs of love-lies-bleeeding emphasise the gathers of the tablecloth.

These two arrangements with their soft, dusky pinks, lilacs and toned-down reds are the epitome of summer and romance. The mixed arrangement in a smart, trumpet-shaped frosted vase is my idea of 'shabby chic' – flowers with a slightly shabby coloration in a chic location. Even though the arrangement is made from fresh flowers it reminds me of old, gently faded botanical prints. The feeling of romance continues with the arrangement of belladonna lilies – clear pastel pink flowers with the most unbelievable soft, soapy fragrance. They have a pure, old-fashioned quality to them that I find completely irresistible.

summer romance

A cluster of belladonna lilies accompanied by the mauveish-purple foliage of *Rosa glauca*, syn. R. *rubrifolia*, stands in a simple but stunning glass vase.

A subdued colour scheme is created by using flag irises in a base of eucalyptus and *Rosa glauca*, syn. *R. rubrifolia*, foliage. There are also clusters of dark purple and lilac-coloured stocks, sprays of 'Sterling Silver' roses, and bursts of washed-out plum-coloured 'Iced Tea' roses.

I do like putting flowers, fruits and other ingredients behind glass or Perspex. It adds another dimension, magnifying and highlighting their colour. Here I filled a glass vase with water then submerged in it whole stems of ornamental red peppers. You can see how the stems are enlarged and their colour enhanced.

red hot peppers

A single stem of peppers in a beer can hanging on a wall looks like a three-dimensional work of art – completely unarranged, yet very effective.

Rising above a glass vase filled with red ornamental peppers, two stems of red heliconia stand tall above a flat collar of *Farfugium japonicum* leaves. The red of this striking arrangement stands out in its monochrome setting, bringing an exotic touch to a very urban environment.

Bright, shiny ornamental peppers have a raw sexiness about them. Their vivid colours look almost painted on, and they are so striking you dare not mix them with anything else. Containers need to be very simple too, so that they are not fighting for attention. The peppers come in different shapes – the red pointed variety used here, which is also available in yellow, orange and an apricot colour, and another variety with small round fruits in orange, yellow and red.

A breath of summer with an arrangement of pastel shades of sweet peas and lady's mantle in a container of cut broom. If you were using it as a table centre for a dinner party, the offcuts of broom could be used to tie up the napkins. Once the broom has dried out, you could use the basket for an autumn arrangement. When buying sweet peas, try to find long-life-treated varieties as these last considerably longer.

Starting with a plain plastic bowl, make a chicken-wire collar, as on page 44. Place the wire collar over a piece of moss that is as deep as the bowl and will wrap around it, then fold the wire around the moss. Fix this moss collar firmly around the bowl with a criss-cross wire. Assemble lengths of broom and use thick wire to hold the ends together in bunches. Wrap the broom bunches around the moss collar and fix with more thick wire. Repeat until the moss is completely covered, using thin wire at intervals to pull the broom in tight against the moss.

Fill the container with crumpled chicken wire, then half-fill with water. Make sure that no moss is hanging over the edges into the container, as this will syphon water off and can cause staining if you place the arrangement on an unprotected surface. You then need to create the foundation of the arrangement. In this case I have used large clusters of lady's mantle. Finish with small bunches of three stems of sweet peas in two or three shades. Fill around the edges first to create a cascading effect, then add more bunches from the top of the arrangement.

a basket of sweet peas

1 Fold chicken wire around a length of moss to make a moss collar and fix the collar around the bowl. 	**2** Wrap bunches of broom around the moss collar, wiring these in to give the effect of a basket of broom. 

3

Place large clusters of lady's mantle into the container to form a solid sturdy base.

4

Create a lush effect, adding bunches of sweet peas first around the edges, then from above.

From the purely classical to the starkly modern, but what unites these two arrangements is the zingy orange and the curvaceous lines of the two vases. The rusty urn's classic shape means that it works really well with the objects around it – the old figurines, the cornucopias and the lions and gryphons. But I think it's the urn's faded grandeur that gives the arrangement its edge. In the case of the single stem of red nerine, part of the arrangement's power comes from the terrific little vase. Its bold colour and simple shape make it a thing of beauty in its own right. Together with the red nerine, it is unbeatable.

sizzling oranges

FAR LEFT AND ABOVE
Tall spikes of *Rosa glauca*, syn.
R. rubrifolia, and of smoke tree
give this warm-toned
arrangement its outline. Depth
is added with the interwoven
clusters of 'Leonardis' roses,
while the orange 'Pareo' roses
give the arrangement more
punch. Whitebeam berries add a
slight autumnal flavour.

This unusual container is plastic, covered with sprigs of box wired in small bunches onto a chicken-wire collar (see page 104). The base is of *Skimmia japonica* 'Rubella', followed by scarlet plume, 'James Storey' orchids and clusters of blood-red 'Black Magic' roses.

red exuberance

You can't beat a whole mass of
Parrot tulips. This variety –
'Estella Rijnveld' – looks really
great edged in the very
characteristic glossy dark green
leaves of *Magnolia grandiflora*,
with their brown suede
undercolour.

The interplay of foliage and flowers makes these two arrangements special. In one, an eruption of
frothy, fringed bi-colour tulips is brought under control by a corset of strict *Magnolia grandiflora*
leaves, tightly tied with raffia. In the other, the exuberance of the arching stems of scarlet plume
and of the 'James Storey' orchids is given free rein. Only the chunky container grounds the
composition. Either arrangement would suit a modern interior, but the juxtaposition of the more
traditional one with the bare loft is slightly unexpected, though none the worse for that.

gerberas

When I go to buy flowers at the market, gerberas are always on my shopping list. I love their strong, open, honest simplicity. There is nothing coy or affected about them. They simply are what they are. Despite their unaffected appearance they are very versatile for flower arranging, looking great either as single blooms – in coloured plastic beakers, they almost look plastic themselves – in single-colour or multi-colour masses, or as the 'star performers' of a mixed arrangement, punctuating it with bold, round splashes of colour. I usually use gerberas as cut flowers, but what fun a mass of mixed plants proves to be, planted in an old wooden trug.

Flower power at its best. Nothing more than a simple bunch of pure white gerberas in a curvy, frosted glass vase, or heads of deep red 'Chateau' gerberas floating in a bowl of silver-lacquered bamboo leaves. Seen close up, the two-tone centres sparkle like the iris of an eye.

Part of the gerbera's versatility lies in its wide range of colours from white to pale pink, red and burgundy through to mid-brown, orange and yellow, and many variations in between. But even the single-colour flowers have touches of contrast, either in the stamens in their centres, or in the tiny petals that sometimes surround the centres. Occasionally a stem will be damaged and the head will droop. If this happens, either cut the stem off and use the flower head on its own – it will look wonderful floating in water – or fix a thick piece of florist's wire into the back of the flower and twist the end around the stem to hold it in place.

a whiter shade of pale

For years it has been argued that white is not a colour, but for me – as well as for that great fashion guru Coco Chanel – white is the best. It is bright and eye-catching, yet also soothing, and looks fabulous on its own but equally good with any other colour. It certainly doesn't need to be boring as no two whites are the same. In fact, in the world of flowers at least, there is no such thing as a pure white. You will find it tinged with yellow, green, pink or blue.

LEFT, FROM TOP
These three flowers all say white, but in totally different ways. The pink-tinged tuberose has a wonderful, romantic perfume, clouds of prunus blossom are a harbinger of spring, while the tiny, tubular white flowers of bells of Ireland hide coyly away in their shell-like calyx.

I don't think you can go wrong with white flowers. They bring purity to any garden design or flower arrangement and, although all-white gardens have long been popular, the minimalist movement has made them especially so in recent years. For me, white tulips are the epitome of minimalist white flowers. I would like nothing more than a mass of them in the centre of my dining table – all year round if that were possible, though I do prefer to use flowers in their correct season.

116

When you look at
this jasmine, with its
beautiful pink-tinged
petals, you can almost
smell its wonderful, heady
fragrance. I always associate
this flower with late spring, as
that is when it is at its best.

For support, the orchids are tied to canes with natural raffia. To maintain this arrangement for as long as possible, keep it out of direct sunlight. As the bowl has no drainage, do not overwater otherwise the young roots will rot.

driftwood & orchids

Pieces of driftwood, together
with the pebbles and the
yellow-beige centres of the
orchids, complement the earth
colours of the abstract painting
in the background.

Orchids, with their beautifully sculpted flowers, bring a touch of exoticism to any room. They
come in colours ranging from hot pink, to green, to the recently introduced chocolate brown. But
to my mind, nothing beats white ones. Here I have planted three white phalaenopsis orchids in a
deep glass bowl. Unless I am using a plant which has an interesting root system, I always like to
line glass bowls with some material such as moss, fruit or bark chippings which are then seen
through the glass. In this case I used some beautiful sea-washed, grey pebbles together with grey
lichen. The final touch was the pieces of weathered driftwood.

agapanthus & swiss cheese

The crisp white of the flowers and the glossy, green leaves work well with the wooden panelling and the old chest of drawers. The arrangement has a strong, smart, colonial feel to it.

Variations on a theme. These two combinations show how, if you are careful, the same ingredients can work in either a small-scale or a large-scale arrangement. I love white agapanthus but it is a very busy-looking flower so needs to be balanced by something with strong, graphic lines. The dark green glossy leaves of the swiss cheese plant fit the bill perfectly. For the vase standing on the small chest of drawers, I have used a small-flowering form of agapanthus – *A.* ‘Bressingham White’ – and small swiss cheese plant leaves. For the striking floor arrangement, a bolder statement was needed, so I used a larger-flowering agapanthus – *A. praecox* subsp. *maximus* ‘Albus’ – and bigger swiss cheese leaves.

This wooden floor needed a
very simple but large-scale
statement. The bold leaves of
the swiss cheese plant provide
the perfect background for a
mass of long white agapanthus
stems in a plain, upright vase.

Here I lined the glass vase with the bold, round leaves of *Farfugium japonicum*, then cut all the stems of the papyrus to the same length to form a radiating dome.

Who needs flowers when we have this wonderful grass? With its strong graphic identity and bright green colour, papyrus is ideally suited to the clean, crisp lines of contemporary interiors. Here I have used it in two very formal arrangements, but a couple of stems placed in a narrow Perspex vase also look terrific – very minimalist. As an added bonus, papyrus also works well when dried, so you can use it twice over. Once dry, it turns a lovely soft sage-green that looks best in a ceramic container.

LEFT, ABOVE
The inspiration for this two-tiered arrangement of papyrus grass was the vase. I trimmed the papyrus to a very exact shape, then broke up the formal lines with some spikes of horsetail. The finished result has a rather oriental feel to it.

papyrus grass

Constance Spry brought the art of flower arranging into the English public eye after the gloomy war years. This shape of vase is very much associated with her, so I wanted to use it for an arrangement in tribute to her. I filled it with a mixture of assorted greenery to show that a perfect display does not necessarily need to include any flowers. The foliages here often appear in my garden designs. Instead of having to prune them at specific times, they can simply be cut as and when they are needed for flower arrangements. They include *Viburnum tinus*, *Hedera canariensis* 'Gloire de Marengo', two types of eucalyptus, mexican orange, *Rosa glauca*, syn. *R. rubrifolia*, *Euonymus japonicus* 'Aureus' and *Brachyglottis* 'Sunshine'.

The varied textures of the different foliages evoke an old-fashioned sense of style that is best suited to a classic interior. With a neutral-coloured container such as this one, you could, if you wanted, add flowers of any colour. I would choose shades of red. Reds and greens always make a successful pairing.

formal foliage

flower-garlanded mirror

Grinling Gibbons was the master of woodcarving and often used his exceptional skills to make frames for paintings or mirrors. He was my inspiration for this design for a classic Victorian bedroom. I hope the garland looks a little as if it is made of carved wood. In order to achieve this effect, I limited myself to using graphic-shaped flowers and even added a few roses made out of wood shavings. The garland also brings out the colours of the small, wooden objects on the mantelpiece. When you choose the frame for your mirror, bear in mind that, by the time you have added the dried flowers, the whole thing will be larger than when you started. Although it may look difficult to make the garland, it is relatively easy and, once it is finished, it will last for many years.

1

Secure wide lengths of chicken wire to a wooden mirror frame with a staple gun.

2

Lay strips of dried moss on top, then fold in the long edges of the wire to hold the moss in place around the frame.

3

Form the wheat into clusters, their stems trimmed to one length, then wire five evenly spaced groups of criss-crossed clusters to the moss.

4

Wire up bunches of single and double feverfew and *Rhodanthe chlorocephalem*, syn. *Helipterum roseum*, and add them next, evenly spaced.

5

Fill in with clusters of dried poppy heads, white peonies, the wood-shaving roses and the white roses.

With their long, slender stems and the edges of their flowers tinged with green, these eucharis look stunning with a necklace of *Hedera canariensis* 'Gloire de Marengo'. The eucharis are excellent as cut flowers. As the flowers fade, remove them and the buds will continue on into bloom.

solo whites

When you are arranging white flowers, you must take special care that the container you use complements the flowers and does not overwhelm them. This square-shaped, metallic vase, narrow at the base and wider at the top, was perfect for the natural, loose look I wanted to achieve with my beautiful bunch of white lilac and eucalyptus. The height of the vase was an added bonus as it meant that I didn't have to cut the lilac down too much. Sadly, lilac does not last very well in an arrangement, but you can improve its chances if you cut the stems at an angle so creating the largest possible surface area to take up water. The frosted vase holding the wonderfully scented eucharis has a heavy base and is tall, which means that it too lends itself to a tall arrangement.

summer celebration

It's always rewarding to be asked to make an arrangement for a special occasion, like this one for a golden wedding. Starting with a simple glass dish like a salad bowl (see page 18), with a ring of wet florist's foam on top, use double-sided tape to fix three glass night-lights in the base, then fill three-quarters full of water and set four church candles in the foam ring. Fill the ring with the foliage, then add the scented white flowers – long spikes of white stocks, groups of three stems of white sweet peas and, finally, clusters of three or five large-headed white 'Tineke' and 'Margaret Merril' roses. I love the way the light from the night-lights ripples out across the table.

LEFT AND BELOW
The foliage base works
perfectly well on its own. To
make it you need variegated
pittosporum, *Brachyglottis*
'Sunshine', cotton lavender,
variegated dracaena and some
gaultheria leaves.

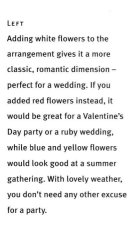

LEFT
Adding white flowers to the
arrangement gives it a more
classic, romantic dimension –
perfect for a wedding. If you
added red flowers instead, it
would be great for a Valentine's
Day party or a ruby wedding,
while blue and yellow flowers
would look good at a summer
gathering. With lovely weather,
you don't need any other excuse
for a party.

LEFT, ABOVE
Large geometric shapes like this lichen tree suit an uncluttered contemporary interior.

LEFT
You could try making a small lichen tree in a galvanised metal pot if the larger one is too daunting.

LEFT
The decoration of this
apartment is a play on circles,
squares and rectangles. A
circular white bowl stands on a
wooden chest, a rectangular
white frame contains a circular
mirror. The palm-leaf tree, plus
the plain white walls, set the
tone for an unusual installation.

RIGHT
Wired-on glass tubes hold white
anthurium flowers. As the
flowers fade they can be
replaced, making an ever-
changing feature.

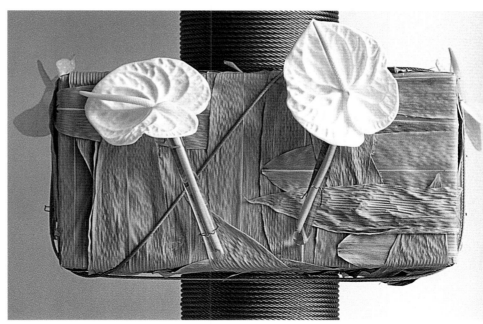

indoor trees

A modern location sometimes demands you be as much an engineering wizard as an arranger of flowers. For my palm-leaf tree, I made the main stem from a piece of plastic piping pushed through three blocks of florist's foam. Next I wrapped the piping in steel cable held on with glue, then covered the foam blocks with palm leaves. The tree is held in place with quick-setting cement in a cube-shaped galvanised container topped with grey lichen. The lichen trees are made from lichen-covered foam. Once again, for the tall tree the stem is wrapped in steel cable and the planter topped off with lichen. These trees are very good for situations with low levels of light, or with only artificial light, where no other tree-sized plant would survive.

This lovely glass test-tube snake, consisting of a metal frame supporting clear glass test tubes, can be manipulated into different shapes. To set it off, I have chosen single stems of white nerines together with a beautiful variegated papyrus folded and tied into loops using raffia. I have also included a few bunches of plain green papyrus, all cut to the same length and again tied with raffia, and have tucked single galax leaves around the stems of some of the nerines so that the leaves show through the glass. The container is supremely versatile. I love it as a centrepiece with narcissi (see page 46), and think it would also look great with blue anemones and sprigs of eucalyptus. It would even lend itself to a Christmas arrangement with red roses and holly.

white nerine snake

In order to emphasise the horizontals in this arrangement, I have taken care to fill the test tubes with water only up to or just above the line of the metal holder. This gives a more interesting look to the stems and leaves, magnifying those that are below the water-line. Clear glass marbles at the bottom of each tube would also look good, especially if you were using flowers such as violets or primulas which have very short stems.

Subtlety and harmony are often the best options for a mixed arrangement, and this one is nothing if not subtle. The foliage is *Magnolia grandiflora*, an evergreen that is often seen as a climber up the walls of old country houses, though it can also be grown as a topiary tree in a small garden. The suede undersides of its leaves have a lovely texture and it is this, plus its colour, that works so well with the chestnuts and walnuts lining the glass bowl. The addition of just one, very choice, type of flower could not be bettered. Originally from Mexico, tuberoses, with their heady fragrance, are among my favourite flowers. Their spiky, architectural flower heads echo the shape of the magnolia leaves. The combined weight of the tuberoses, with their heavy heads, the foliage and the water is quite substantial, so you must make sure that you use florist's tape to stick the plastic bowl carefully in place inside the glass container, otherwise everything may topple over.

tuberoses & nuts

1

Stand a rigid plastic bowl in the centre of a glass dish, fix the bowl in position using florist's tape, then add water.

2

Put some crumpled chicken wire in the plastic bowl then line the space between the bowl and the glass with alternating panels of walnuts and chestnuts.

3

Fill in with a base of *Magnolia grandiflora* leaves.

4

Finally, add single stems of tuberoses, evenly spaced throughout the foliage.

At the height of summer, what could be more delightful than a hat decorated with blowsy, scented old garden roses? This design needs the flower heads to be wired up individually, then made into a garland to be placed around the crown of the hat. Once finished, keep it cool and out of direct sunlight until you are ready to wear it.

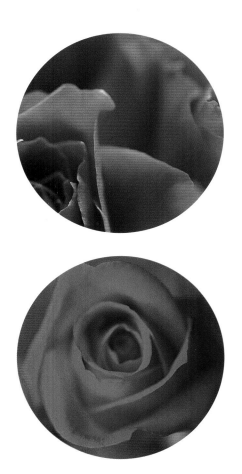

roses

Roses are one of the earliest cultivated flowers. In Roman times they stood for intrigue and celebration. It is said that the emperor Nero's extravagance with roses was one of the causes of the collapse of the Roman empire. Nowadays, roses – especially red ones – are usually associated with romance. In summer I love giving and receiving bunches of garden roses, and when I am designing a garden I always try to include some, preferably shrub roses whose large blooms add great strength to any border. My favourites are 'Buff Beauty' and 'Felicia'. The mauve-purple foliage of *Rosa glauca*, syn. *R. rubrifolia*, is another must for any garden.

'Margaret Merril' roses and the green spray rose, *R.* x *odorata* 'Viridiflora', are so special that they do not need any accompaniment. Here I grouped a whole mass of them together without any foliage and placed them in a very simple, rectangular frosted vase. I hope this conveys the idea of a traditional English rose garden at the height of summer.

What could be simpler yet more elegant and opulent than this mass of lovely pinkish-white, heavenly scented 'Heritage' garden roses? Artlessly arranged in an old, cut-glass container, they look classic on a marble-topped cabinet with a statuette and the cloud print.

Acknowledgments

Putting this book together has been such a lovely experience. Without such a strong team to help, none of it would have been possible. Firstly, a big, heartfelt thank you to Lorry Eason who has taken all the brilliant pictures and who was the most calming influence on me on shoot days. I think you will agree that her photographs have a wonderful depth and magic. Secondly, thank you to Françoise Dietrich, the most wonderful art director and designer who happens to share my passion for food. She helped me choose many of the locations and came to understand my love of flowers. Thanks to her, the pages of this book have been put together in a very unique and original way. The award for patience and understanding has to go to Hilary Mandleberg, the editor, without whom the book would not have had any words, nor would it have met the deadline. Thanks too, to the team at Quadrille, especially Jane O'Shea, whose encouragement and support made this book happen.

I would also like to thank all my family, friends, colleagues and clients who have given me so much encouragement and help during the twelve months we were putting this book together. These include Chrissie Rouffignac, Keith Brymer Jones, Mark Watty and Rosbie Morton. Thanks also to Emma Townsend and Dierdre Taylor, my P.A.s, who made sure I turned up on time and at the right place, and to Heather Alexander who covered for me at work whenever it was necessary.

At Covent Garden Market I would like to thank Alan Gardiner and all his team at Alagar; Dennis, Ted, Andy and John Painter at Page Monro; Bob Palmer and Charlie French and their team of porters at A.W. Carey; Barry with his endless selection of foliage at Ronald Porter; David and John Egan for their continued support; Dennis Edwards at David Austin; Terry Dicker and Martin Punter at Arnott & Mason; Craig Broadley and Dave Knight at Quality Plants; Reg Wisbey at Something Special; C. Best and J. Ray and all the team at Evergreen.

Publishers' acknowledgments

The publishers would like to thank the following for the use of their homes: Robert Dye and Lucinda Sebag-Montefiore, whose home was designed by Robert Dye Associates, pages 40–41, 113, 118–19, 129; Mary Evans, pages 16 (left), 17, 68–9, 104–5; Richard Fyfe, pages 16 (centre), 54–5, 98–9, 111, 130–31, 141 (bottom); Lawrence Isaacson, interior design by Peter Leonard, pages 18, 66–7, 74–5, 76–7, 82, 136–7; Nik Randall, Suszi Corio and Louis, whose home was designed by Brookes Stacey Randall, pages 44–5, 78, 85, 93, 94–5, 109, 112, 128; Andrew and Marie Sorrell, pages 15 (bottom), 16 (right), 19 (left), 42, 43, 48–9, 50–51, 52–3, 91, 100–101, 106–7, 120–21, 124–5, 126–7, 140, 141 (top); and Libby Sellors, pages 38 (centre), 47, 70–71, 108. They would also like to thank Owain George for the loan of the chair (page 97), William Yeoward for the loan of the vase (page 47), Fianne Stanford from Kirker Greer Candles for the loan of the candles (pages 44–5), Tony Lord for help with the plant nomenclature, Tessa Clark for editorial assistance and Geoff Wilkinson for the cover photograph of the author.

Index